Singing Down the Breadfruit

Singing Down the Breadfruit

PAULINE STEWART

Illustrated By
Duncan Smith

The Bodley Head
London

Copyright © text Pauline Stewart 1993
Copyright © illustrations Duncan Smith 1993

The rights of Pauline Stewart and Duncan Smith to be
identified as the author and illustrator of this work
have been asserted by them in accordance with the Copyright,
Designs and Patents Act, 1988.

First published in 1993 by
The Bodley Head Children's Books
an imprint of Random House UK Ltd
20 Vauxhall Bridge Road, London SW1V 2SA

Random House Australia Pty Ltd
20 Alfred Street, Sydney, NSW 2061

Random House New Zealand Ltd
PO Box 40–086, Glenfield, Auckland 10, New Zealand

Random House South Africa Pty Ltd
PO Box 337, Bergvlei 2012, South Africa

Typeset by Deltatype Ltd, Ellesmere Port
Printed and bound in Great Britain

A catalogue record for this book
is available from the British Library

ISBN 0–370–31824 2

CONTENTS

For my family, especially my mother Enid and daughter, Leila.
Also many thanks to Anne McNeil and Caroline Thomas
and colleagues at Random House.

Island Necklace

The Caribbean islands form a
necklace in the sea.
At night they look like diamonds;
daytime, emeralds to me.

Tropical Rain

When rain falls it falls
warmly and suddenly
                in large drops
       Over mountain
        Over sea
HEAVY RAIN can turn streets
               swiftly
into rivers.
Rain pours
on to roofs and into gutters
fills up all the water tanks
runs
       down
          shutters.
Rain brings out bright umbrellas.
When it rains the earth is drinking.

Gilbert

I hope that he'll not come again
that nasty Mister Hurricane.

You see that man is not polite
he sent farm animals into flight
and every time that man did sneeze
he bent back zinc and ripped up trees.
He took his claws and scratched the land
cleaned his nails and sprinkled sand.

I hope that he'll not come again
that nasty Mister Hurricane.

He ate us out of house and home
disconnected light and phone
and when he had enough of fun
left as quickly as he'd come.

I hope that he'll not come again
that nasty Mister Hurricane.

Fruit Cocktail

Dice up the mango do!
Make triangles of pineapples
stir in the cherries too
slices of banana
segments of kiwi green
add some pear put guava there
twelve curls of tangerine.

One Away

We had six goats
now only five leave . . .
Seem like smaddy carry it
weh up dem sleeve.
Perhaps goaty did decide
to trot up the road –
let sun catch him hide.
Like how goat
can't join navy
maybe someone capture him
to make up gravy.
GOATY! GOATY!

Corn Song

Corn growing in the big field,
Cornrow in my hair,
Corn on granny's little toe,
Cornmeal in the air.

Sauce

Aunt Ruth came from England
and guess all that we got –
a jar of English mustard
which she said was very hot.

'That yellow thing no pepper!'
remarked my aunty Dot.
'England famous for it strawberry
but for pepper it is not!'

Before we could prevent her
Aunt D dip in she big spoon.
It hot! it hot! so till
it nearly send her to the moon.

Now aunty Dot eats quietly
she scarcely speaks a word
she no touch the jar of mustard
since it deaden she taste-bud.

Washday

In the sun we scrips our clothes
and everyone around us knows
that soon our sheets will sail the wind
flap and flutter, twirl like string.
Our tops and bottoms look like flags
hung on a line which gently sags.
The washday chore is almost done
my jeans dry quickly in the sun.

Dance

I love to dance dance
juk up juk up me shoulders
twissy twassy me waist
scrinchy scrinch up me face
bouncy me feet to the beat
I love to dance dance
would you like to join me?

Christmas in the Sun

I like when Christmas time is here
I like to welcome the New Year
I like the pretty coloured lights
hung outside on Christmas night.
This year,
I hope Santa will make a mistake
and shower us all in cool snowflakes.

The Bully

You know it's quite a mystery
why Glenford likes to bully me
when I've done nothing at all
he pushes me and then I fall.
At playtime sitting on the benches
he showers me with spiteful punches.
Teacher, Teacher can't you see?
How Glenford Lewis bullies me?
He says that if I ever tell
both my cheeks are sure to swell.
Things could not get much worse . . .
so I think I'll tell my parents first.

Cricket

Some day I'm going to be excellent at cricket.
One day my runs will go down in history.
I'll strike the ball beyond the boundary.
I'll send it clear into another country.

Welcome to the Craft Market

Come in come in and see
our hands have been busy
making fine jewellery, weaving fancy baskets,
carving wooden faces, painting sunny places.
Plenty things we have in store
step inside we will show you more.
Need a key-ring or straw hat?
We have ornaments for house or flat.
What? you like the sandal shoe?
I'll make it cheaper just for you.

Lazy

How dare they
call me lazy
when all the things
that I have done
are scattered

                everywhere?

The fact that
they still
need doing
is
neither

                here

nor

                there.

Riddle

It is not always carnival
for all play must have an interval.

It is not always honey juice
or either what we'd like to choose.

It is not always friends to love us,
neither the comfort of our mothers.

It is not always bright parades
sometimes it's mellow, lonely shades.

But what it is, is Life!

The Star's Pillow

I thought the star had disappeared
but it had not really.
There it's blinking through the cloud
I see it now quite clearly.

A Country Bus Ride

A country bus chugs through
the early morning mist and dew
its rattling machinery
wakes up the drowsy scenery
dreamily we wait.
There's no mistaking that horn,
a sound to warn drivers
on the other side of corners.
We board,
a laughing pushing horde
we crowd on to the bus.
A few dollars will take you far
as good as any taxi or car.
'One stop driver' comes the shout.
Five get in only one jumps out.
Whether you're heading to school,
work or town,
be glad if you arrive
without a single breakdown.

Singing Down the Breadfruit

Her father blended truth and myth
so finely that each became the other.
'Well' he would start,
'fac is fac . . . is fac dat we is
good singers – right?'
– 'Ee-hee.' She would reply.
'Well is for a purpose.'
– 'What purpose, poopa?'
'See how coconut tree tallaway,
swipple an' hard fe scale?'
– 'Ee-hee.'
'Well, when we cyan go no more,
we jus' sing dung de coconut,
sing dung de mangoes an' de breadfruit dem.'
'Sing dem dung?'
'Yes, all de way
dung
to
de
grung.'
– 'like de wind?'
'Jus like de wind.'

Penfriend

I'm writing my friend a letter.
She lives across the sea
I hope that she'll come over
and visit my family.
I wonder what sights she sees
I wonder what she does.
I suppose really
she's more or less like us.
All kinds of people
live in the world today.
I wonder if they wrote to me
exactly what they'd say?

Baby Blues

Hushhhhhhhh. . .
These ain't tears my honey
no sir these ain't tears
these be diamonds baby
these be diamonds dear.

The Surprise Party

'Quick! Quick!' whispers Mum
'I hear the car, I think he's come!'
Lights out! Music off!
Mum's not quite certain
whether or not
he'll see us through
the net curtain.
While we wait
for Dad to park
we giggle and
whisper in the dark.
Jo-Jo calls, 'That's him
I know that coat . . .
suppose he smells
the curry goat?!'
We laugh but Uncle Dudley
sucks his teeth:
'But wait! It looks to me
like him did forget him key!'
Patricia and Mikey
begin to row
they suggest
we open the door
right now.
Sshhhhhh!
At last we hear
Dad fumble
with the door,
Mum says, 'Wait for the
count of four.'
– A pause

silence
then the shrug
of shadowed shoulders
the air is tense
none of us can take
the suspense.
Suddenly the door
flies open
the birthday spell
abruptly broken.
It's Dad who shouts
'SURPRISE!'
Just like Dad
he knew all along
and now he's
whistling the
birthday song!

Mountain Moon and Gold

Grandmother is getting slower and complains
that her heart clock is running late.
Grandfather slaps her on the bottom and laughs
that no matter how old
she has not even begun
to catch up mountain moon and gold.

The Clock

Our clock does not tick tock
neither does it keep good time
the hands are way too fast
it seems not to know when to chime.
Last week (the exact time I forget)
we all rushed to school – it wasn't open yet!

Next Door's Cat

In the holidays we take care
of next door's cat Tiger who is now
so fat that she barely squeezes
through her own cat flap.

She thinks she's the cat's pyjamas
she does she does
She thinks she's the cat's pyjamas
she does.

No matter how much you call
she'll pay you no mind at all
she'll stay on the fence by the apple tree
pretending she's deaf and she cannot see.

She thinks she's the cat's pyjamas
she does she does
She thinks she's the cat's pyjamas
she does.

Give her a cushion if you please
your bed, the sofa, but not your knees
she is far too proud for that
she'll flick flack off like an acrobat.

She thinks she's the cat's pyjamas
she does she does
She thinks she's the cat's pyjamas
she does she does.

Last week she gave us all a heart attack
by darting in front of a blue Fiat
and although she really is not mine
she seems to be here all the time.

But
She thinks she's the cat's pyjamas
she does she does
She thinks she's the cat's pyjamas
she does she does.

Jigsaw Trees

Winter's coming.
The trees lose their leaves in cold breezes.
Like pieces of a jigsaw puzzle
they scatter around and
only spring knows how
to put them back together again.

Night Creatures

Lizards licking
crickets cricking
bats flapping
snakes slipping
owls scowl
dogs howl
chickens flurry
mongoose hurry
spiders sneaking
frogs creaking
mosquitoes sipping
rats ripping.
'GOODNIGHT!'

Blue Bottle

Fly! Fly! Don't you dare
pitch 'pon me!
I've warned you already
if you do you'll see.
Flying around town
turning good food bad
the sound of you alone
is driving me mad.
Fly! Fly! Don't you dare
pitch 'pon me
If you do you'll see
I'll squash you flat
or spray you – now
how would you like that?

Skinny Street

Nearby there runs
a skinny street
with rows of skinny
houses neat
which all have skinny
little ledges
behind some
skinny squashed in
hedges.
Skinny lampposts
Skinny trees
Skinny litter
in a skinny breeze.
Sometimes a skinny
ray of light
falls on a bicycle
black and bright.
Sometimes skinny
raindrops fall.
And
on a good market day
all kinds of people
Use the
skinny
alley-way.

Two Different Things

When I was three or four
perhaps even much smaller
I used to think bread
came from a breadfruit tree . . .
and that bakeries
wrapped them up you see.
I believed all that was said
about rolls, pastries and bread.
It really didn't matter though
because I soon saw for myself
a baker wrestle with dough.

Goodbye Granny

Goodbye Granny
it's nearly time to fly
goodbye Granny
I am going in the sky.
I have my suitcase
and things.
You have packed
me everything
except the sunshine.
All our good times
are stored
up inside
more than enough
for any plane ride.
Goodbye Granny
things will be all right
goodbye Granny
I won't forget to write.
Goodbye Granny
bye! bye!
bye! bye!

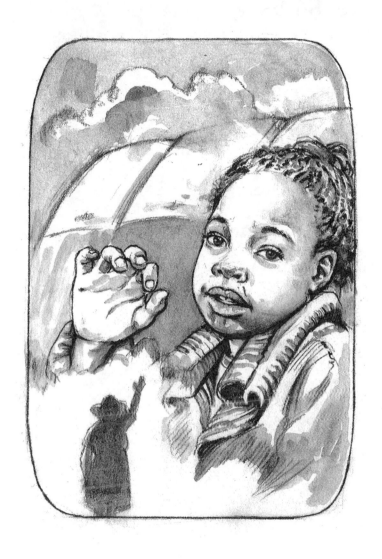

Planet So-So

Imagine a planet
    far out in space
               where
one kind of people
                  live
in one kind of
          place.
One kind of
             language,
one kind of flower,
  days which last for
only one hour.
    This planet has
                 one
so-so star.
The people there
play
one-string
            guitars.
The So-so people tell
one
    so-so joke
about a cold cup
                    of
tea
      and
          an artichoke.
The weather
            forecast
     is always bleak,
    beneath their
so-so cloud called
         Unique.

Our Allotment

They often say 'Here is not like over there.'
My parents, who remember
when they were so much younger
tending their ground, planting a tree
hearing the wind in the sugar cane
sounding like sea.

'Here is not like over there,
here is quick, quick, there is slow.'
Except in the winter when frost and snow
keep us indoors,
avoiding all our gardening chores.

But in the spring they like it here
when flowers are opening everywhere.
Then they, with more enjoyment,
take extra pride in the allotment.

Even when they have grown grey hair
they'll still say, 'Here is not like over there.'
Over there they would have a few flying fish
to put with the potatoes which they call 'irish'
and also they would serve dasheen and yam
vegetables more common in their homeland.
They say the earth there smells of rust
that certain plants are poisonous but
me I have never been
across to see what they have seen
so I make do until I do with digging our allotment.

Bath

Wash wash in the bath
even though I'm not dirty.
If I keep on washing every day
I'll be clean by the time I'm thirty.

Out of Work

Julie used to go to work
Julie used to
wear clean blouse and fancy skirt
Julie used to
jump up quick as she could
Julie used to
without even eating food
Julie used to jump on tube
Julie used to dash about
sometimes Julie took me out
now all the raindrops in the sky
seem to be in Julie's eye.

Where Duppy Deh?

Duppy live in de sun?
Ghost deh a Englan'?
Me no believe ina
neither one a dem!

Note: a duppy is a type of Caribbean ghost.

Sleep

Sleep is a shy dancer
who hides
most of the day away.
Sleep is sometimes heavy
sometimes light
like a blanket
spread at night
pressing down on tired bodies.

Skin

Teacher says I have many colours in my skin.
Some colours are thick. Some colours are thin.
I have a bit of everything mixed in . . .
browns, whites, blacks, pinks too
some of my veins are a greeny blue.
Teacher said it is a sad fact
that so many people only ever see black.

Angel Cake
(on special offer)

What a trick!
What a gimmick!
The one we bought
had nothing in it!

Garden Zoo

In my dream I had a garden zoo
with lions, tigers and a pink cockatoo.
Zebras and elephants were roaming there
while chimpanzees swung through the air.
Dolphins and seals swam to and from
the banks of the pond (turned aquarium).
An alligator, giraffe and a kangaroo
were there as guests in the garden too.
Now and then, the most colourful plants,
tempted a doctor bird to dance.
Then I fed the animals green calliloo,
yes they loved to eat green calliloo
and wash it down with red bean stew.
In my dream I had a garden zoo
will I dream of it tomorrow too. . . ?

Seamstress

The Singer sang
and the Pfaff
pfaffed out
seas of garments
while my mother
at the helm
shaped the
fabric of our lives.

Miss Jessica and Sugar

Miss Jessica love sugar is a shame
Miss Jessica know every sweetie name
Miss Jessica no 'fraid diabetes
Miss Jessica keep sucking sweeties
Miss Jessica brush off all coconut drop
Miss Jessica gwaps down soursop
Miss Jessica no have sweet tooth tho'
she lef dem dung de dentist long time ago.

Fine Combs

Fine combs specialize in chewing hair.
Fine combs specialize in rip and tear.
Fine combs love to leave just one strand there.
Fine combs grin from hair to ear.
Fine combs with fine teeth don't care.
Fine combs only like fine hair.

Muddah How You No Tired A Me Yet?

Muddah how you no tired a me yet?
wid all the things I do feget
like no fe slam door
and always a bother you fe more.
And muddah please do fegive me
for thinking you is Christmas tree
when 'de best things in life free'
like fe we own natural history.
So muddah if you tell me more
I'll stay inside and close the door.

Stranger in the Hall

It's just a hat and coat I know
but in the darkness it's not at all,
more like a stranger in the hall.
S/he does not talk or move at all
just loiters downstairs in the hall.

As I go by, I flick the switch
And never detect a single twitch.
But always just before I go
I tend to whisper 'friend or foe?'

Maroons

My mother's mother told her and now she tells me
about the great warrior queen Nanny.
There were other leaders too,
such as Johnny, Accompong, Cudjoe,
Kishee, Quacu and Quao.

*Note: During the time of slavery, escaped groups of mainly
African slaves banded together to fight enslavement on the
plantations in Jamaica. These groups took to the inaccessible
mountains from where they attacked. They are believed to have
got their name originally from the Spanish term cimarron, a
word describing livestock which had escaped and reverted to
being wild. In Jamaica, the Maroons eventually signed peace
treaties. Nanny and Cudjoe are national heroes in Jamaica. I
have placed Nanny in prominence because my mother is
descended from the Moore Town Maroons, a group she ruled.*

Golden Beach

                    All the while
people talk about our golden beaches
stretching coast to coast through rocky reaches.
On the radio we hear
from glossy brochures pictures stare.
Mum and Dad will take us there,
where gold, as common as sand,
is available to every hand
and I will wade in up past my waist
. . . while bathers sleep I'll fill my case . . .

New Boy

Today
everyone is laughing
at your long name
and your skinny legs
which look like
two burnt out matches
but by next week
I bet
they'll be your friends.

Poor Anancy

When Dad steps on spiders
Mum whispers 'poor Anancy'.

Little Bird

My sister and I once
found a bird with
a broken wing.
We did not say a
word to our parents
when we should have.
Instead we tried
to mend it with
the softest wood
we could find.
We tied it with
a piece of string,
we fed that bird
everything and
squeezed droplets of
milk between its beak
but the bird was weak.
So we left it on
a tray of straw,
the next day we
planned to do more.
The following morning
we rose as the
day was dawning
only to find
the bird gone.
My sister said
the bird must
have died
but me I like
to think that   it flied.

Humming Birds and Bees

Humming birds and bees both like pollen
and another thing they have in common
is humming all the words they have forgotten.

Birdsong Lullaby

As evening comes and blue light tints the sky
sleepily I listen for the birdsong lullaby.
Waiting by my window I feel the cool twilight,
hear the fidgeting of insects
who love to dance at night.
Then begins the singing, especially for me.
One bird's little solo becomes a choir tree.
'Chirr-up!', 'Chirr-up!', 'Cheer up!',
they seem to say.
Put drowsy head on pillow
while we sing the day away.

Old Songs

Old songs do not die
they drift on up
they linger high
into the atmosphere
where
they whisper into lonely ear.
Old songs are always there,
they strain right up
towards the moon
then tinkle down
upon new tunes.

Index of Titles

Index of First Lines